Beyond the Mirror

HENRI J.M. NOUWEN

Beyond the Mirror

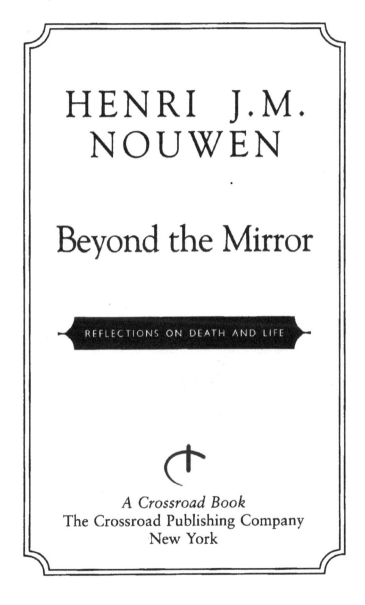

REFLECTIONS ON DEATH AND LIFE

A Crossroad Book
The Crossroad Publishing Company
New York

This printing: February 2016

The Crossroad Publishing Company
www.crossroadpublishing.com

Copyright © 1990 by Henri J. M. Nouwen
This edition published 2001 by The Crossroad Publishing Company
Foreword copyright © 2001 by Robert Durback
"Preparing for Death" © 2001 by The Estate of Henri J. M. Nouwen

Printed in the United States of America

Library of Congress Cataloging-in-Publication Data

Nouwen, Henri J. M.
    Beyond the mirror : reflections on death and life / by Henri J.M.
Nouwen.
       p. cm.
    Originally published: 1990.
    ISBN 978-0-8245-1961-2 (alk. paper)
    1. Death – Religious aspects – Christianity. 2. Accidents – Religious
aspects – Christianity. 3. Spiritual life – Christianity. 4. Nouwen,
Henri J. M. I. Title.
BT825 .N66 2002
236'.1 – dc21

                                                      2001002775

Contents

5

Acknowledgments

This story could never have been published without the generous support and secretarial help of Connie Ellis and the dedicated editorial assistance of Conrad Wieczorek and Phil Zaeder. To the three of them I want to express my deep gratitude.

Foreword

There is something enchanting about mirrors. Storytellers understand their power to capture the imagination of children, to lead them into the realm of mystery. We gaze into mirrors to see what we look like, to discover who we are. The brothers Grimm understood this. The queen in Snow White consults with her mirror to seek reinforcement of her self-image: "Mirror, mirror, on the wall, who is the fairest one of all?" When the queen does not get the answer she wants, in a fit of rage she lets go of what beauty she has and exchanges it instead for the ghastly features of an ugly old witch. The story invites us to ponder before our own looking glasses.

The special appeal of Henri Nouwen has been his consistency in his writings in offering himself as a foil, holding up to his readers his own lived experience as a reflecting glass, as it were, into which we can gaze and probe the deeper dimensions of who we are, a mirror into which we can look and discover ourselves anew, both in our vulnerabilities, but also in our hidden potential, our true destinies.

In *Beyond the Mirror* Nouwen gives us an account of an accident in which he was seriously injured when struck by the outside rearview mirror of a passing van as he was hitchhiking on a dark winter morning laden with heavy snow and ice along the roadside. More importantly, the book gives us an account of his reflections as he found himself close to death and awaiting surgery in the emergency room of a hospital in Toronto, and his subsequent thoughts on the experience in the days following his recovery.

Face to face with death, Nouwen had to sort out what was really important about the life he had lived and the small slice of life left to him now, as he faced the possibility of imminent death. As the reader follows Nouwen step by step through the logic of negotiating with death, the reader, too, is inevitably drawn into the process of sorting out ultimate values, weighing decisions in the present about what really matters, not waiting for the moment when time runs out and new decisions are no longer an option.

Ordinarily death is a subject we do not find particularly inviting. We would rather avoid it altogether, lest it cast a shadow on our lives. In this new edition of *Beyond the Mirror*, however, Nouwen shows us how the awareness of our mortality can in fact enrich our lives. The very fact of the shortness of our lives reminds us of how precious every moment is. Few of us are so well off financially that we can afford to throw our spare money away. If we would stop to think about it, neither can any of us afford to throw the spare years of our lives away, rationed out to us, as they are, only day by day and moment by moment.

For Nouwen death itself became a mirror that brought him face to face with the question: "Who am I?" Over a lifetime we acquire many identities: I am what I do. I am what I have. I am a mother. I am a father. I am single and lonely. I am a sales clerk. I am a marketing analyst. I'm an artist. I'm unemployed. Sadly, so many might be inclined to say: "I'm a nobody."

Nouwen, as he lay dying in the hospital, could have said to himself: I'm a theologian, I'm a psychologist, I've taught at Yale and Harvard, I've written many books, I've lectured nationally and internationally. But these were not the thoughts that brought him comfort in what he perceived to be his final hour. Death strips away the many superficial layers of identity we wear.

12

Which of his many identities brought Nouwen comfort as he lay suspended between life and death? What sense of self finally trumped all other cards in his life? As he peers into the mirror of his life to search for the definitive answer to the question "Who am I?" he hears these words spoken directly to him: "This is my beloved Son, with whom I am well pleased" (Matthew 3:17). Nouwen hears these words not spoken to Jesus alone, but to himself and to all humanity represented in Jesus: "I know now," he says, "that the words spoken to Jesus when he was baptized are words spoken also to me and to all who are brothers and sisters of Jesus."

He concludes: "My tendencies toward self-rejection and self-depreciation make it hard to hear these words truly and let them descend into the center of my heart. But once I have received these words fully, I am set free from my compulsion to prove myself to the world and can live in it without belonging to it. Once I have accepted the truth that I am God's beloved child, unconditionally loved, I can be sent into the world to speak and to act as Jesus did....I am convinced that I will truly be able to love the world when I fully believe that I am loved far beyond its boundaries."

By sharing with his readers in this intensely personal account the full sweep of his own self-understanding in the face of death, Nouwen frees the rest of us from the very constricted, narrow, false identities we craft for ourselves, abetted by the media and its flood of hollow advertising. Led by Nouwen, we can walk through our mirrors into the real world of our true selfhood, designed by a loving God and destined for a future beyond our imagining.

ROBERT DURBACK

Prologue

This little book is a spiritual story about an accident, one that I suffered myself. I have written it because I had no choice. My accident brought me to the portal of death and led me to a new experience of God. Not writing about it would have been unfaithful to my vocation to proclaim the presence of God at all times and in all places. Books and articles have been important in my search for God, but it has been the interruptions to my everyday life that have most revealed to me the divine mystery of which I am a part.

A long time of solitude in a Trappist monastery interrupting a busy life of teaching, the sudden death of my mother interrupting my deepest bond with my family, a confrontation with poverty in Latin America interrupting a rather comfortable life in the North, a call to live with mentally handicapped people interrupting an academic career, the breakage of a deep friendship interrupting a growing sense of emotional safety—such events have forced me over and over again to ask myself the question "Where is God and who is God for me?"

All of these interruptions presented themselves as opportunities to go beyond the normal patterns of daily life and find deeper connections than the previous safeguards of my physical, emotional, and spiritual well-being. Each interruption invited me to look in a new way at my identity before God. Each interruption took something away from me; each interruption offered something new. Beyond the success of teaching was the inner peace of solitude and community; beyond the bond with my mother was the maternal presence of God; beyond the comforts of North America were the smiles of the children of God in Bolivia and Peru; beyond the academic career was the vocation to touch God in those whose minds and bodies are broken; beyond a very nurturing friendship was the communion with a God who asked for every part of my heart. In short, beyond the many "social arrangements" that make for a good life are the many possibilities of a relationship with the God of Abraham and Sarah, Isaac and Rebekah, Jacob, Leah and Rachel, the Father of Jesus, whose name is Love.

These many interruptions calling me "beyond" compelled me to write. First of all, I was compelled simply because writing seemed the only way for me not to lose heart in the frightening and often devastating interruptions and to hold on to my innermost self while moving from known to unknown places. Writing helped me to remain somewhat focused amid the turmoil and to discern

17

better the small guiding voice of God's Spirit in the midst of the cacophony of distracting voices. But there was always a second motivation. Somehow I believed that writing was one way to let something of lasting value emerge from the pains and fears of my little, quickly passing life. Each time life required me to take a new step into unknown spiritual territory, I felt a deep, inner urge to tell my story to others—perhaps as a need for companionship but maybe, too, out of an awareness that my deepest vocation is to be a witness to the glimpses of God I have been allowed to catch.

When I was hit by a van while hitchhiking and found myself, soon after, faced with the possibility of death, I felt more than ever that what I was living then I had to live for others. Since I have returned to health and am able to tell my story, I feel that this interruption, which could have been the last, gave me a new knowledge of God that contrasted radically with what I had learned so far. And so, more strongly than ever before, I feel a need to write about it and simply present this knowledge I cannot keep for myself alone.

I hope and pray that this glimpse beyond the mirror will bring comfort and hope to my brothers and sisters who are afraid to think of their approaching death, or who think of it in fear and trembling, but never in peace.

The Accident

The Accident

TWO VIVID RECOLLECTIONS remain in me of that moment on a dark winter morning when the outside rearview mirror of a passing van struck me in the back and flung me to the ground beside the road. I knew at once that I had reached a point of no return. I did not know how seriously I was injured, but I knew that something old had come to an end and that something new, as yet unknown, was about to emerge.

As I lay by the side of the busy road, crying for help, I knew also from the instant I was hit that this was not purely an accident. Later I would be able to see clearly how predictable, providential, and mysteriously planned the whole event was. At the time, my primary concern was that help would arrive, yet I realized that something strangely "good" was happening as I lay on the side of the road.

It had been a very busy week, filled with many little things, none of them terribly important, but still taking up every hour of my time and leaving me quite tired, even somewhat irritated. There never seemed to be the space to come into direct touch with my own inner source. There was, however, one clear exception. I had been asked to help Hsi-Fu, a deeply handicapped fourteen-year-old Chinese boy, to get ready for school in the mornings. Nathan and Todd, who usually help Hsi-Fu, had left to participate in a retreat, and I was very glad to take their place.

In fact, I felt quite privileged to have the opportunity of coming close to Hsi-Fu. Hsi-Fu is blind, unable to speak or walk, and has both physical and intellectual disabilities; but he is so full of life and love that being with him helps me to get in touch with what it is that makes life so truly nurturing. Bathing him, brushing his teeth, combing his hair, and just guiding his hand as he tries to put some food on his spoon and bring it to his mouth create a safe intimacy, a quiet bond, a moment of true peace—almost like an hour of meditation. I had already spent Monday, Tuesday, and Wednesday mornings going through his routine with him, and I looked forward to being with him again.

Hsi-Fu lives in the so-called Corner House in downtown Richmond Hill, a five-minute drive from the house in which I stay. That Thursday morning I woke up early, and when I looked out of the window, I saw that the ground had become a sheet of shining ice. Obviously, it would be impossible to drive the half mile from the house out to Yonge Street. The dirt road had become more fit for skating than driving, and taking the car would only land me in a ditch.

My friend Sue, who was on her way to prayer when I was ready to leave, said, "Don't take your car out. It's impossible." I said, "No, no, I will walk. It's only six o'clock and I will easily get there by seven." Sue replied, "Henri, don't go. It's too much. Call the Corner House; they'll find a solution' for Hsi-Fu." Right then I felt a deep resistance to letting go of what I so much wanted to do. Again Sue said, "Don't go." But I persisted, "I can do it. I promised." So I left the house and began shuffling my way over the icy road out to Yonge Street.

Walking proved difficult, and at one point I slipped and fell flat on my stomach. But I kept saying to myself, "Keep going. You can make it. Don't let a little ice get in your way." It was not pure service that motivated me now but the desire to show myself that I could fulfill a little task, and the even stronger desire to let no one take Hsi-Fu away from me, at least for this week.

When I reached Yonge Street, I saw that it had taken me fifteen minutes to get there. I crossed the road and began walking south to Richmond Hill. As I walked, I began to feel very anxious. Cars were streaming by, and although the road itself seemed free of ice, the shoulders were very dangerous. I kept stumbling and coming close to falling. When I reached the gas station, I realized that it was already half past six and that I would be unable to make it to the Corner House by seven.

Just then, a small truck with two men inside pulled into the station. I decided to ask their help. I knocked on the truck window, and when the man sitting beside the driver rolled it down, I said, "Good morning. Is there any chance that you could take me downtown? I have to be there at seven o'clock, and with all the ice on the shoulder of the road, I'm never going to make it. It's only a three-minute drive." The driver leaned over toward me and said, "No, we can't help you. We're just arriving to open the station. We have no time."

I decided to try again. "Listen, it's only a few minutes, and I really feel nervous walking along the road with all this ice. Please, can you help me? It won't take you very long." But the answer was the same: "I'm sorry, we have no time." I started to feel anger rising in me and a strange desire to force these men into helping me. So I said, "But I really have to be over there"—I pointed with my hand—"where you can see the church tower, and I won't make it if you don't help me. There's nobody here who needs you right now." The driver started to back his truck further into the parking area, saying, "I'm sorry, we have no time. We have to open the shop." Meanwhile, his passenger closed the window and left me alone.

Suddenly I felt very angry. These two complete strangers had become my enemies. I felt indignation, yes, even rage erupting from a deep, dark place within me. I had been misunderstood, pushed aside, rejected, and left alone. A feeling like that of an abandoned child swept through me. Turning toward the street, along the shoulder, I knew I had to be careful, but I wasn't. I trudged where cars with glaring headlights were speeding by one after the other. Now I was determined to be on time. I would show that pair that I could do without them, that I didn't really need them, that other people would show more compassion than they, and that, after all, I was right and they were wrong.

As I approached the moving traffic, I turned to the oncoming headlights and raised my right hand, pointing toward downtown Richmond Hill. Car after car emerged from the morning mist and passed me by. I thought about all those men and women driving comfortably to work alone in their cars and, peevishly, began wondering why no one seemed to notice me or show any inclination to stop and take me the little distance I needed to go. The two enemies had become many.

A strange ambiguity had me in its grip. My mind understood clearly that in these conditions it was completely unrealistic to expect a passing driver to see me, realize that I needed help, and stop and take me downtown. I certainly would never be able to do all of that were I driving to work at half past six in the morning of an icy day. Despite this, there was, at the same time, this rage, this increasing feeling of rejection, this inner shriek: "Why do you all pass me by, ignore my pleas, and leave me standing alone on the side of the road?" My insight into the absurdity of my expectations kept intersecting with my strange anger.

Finally I decided that the only way to make it to the Corner House was to walk. Meanwhile, though, time had passed and provided no chance for me to reach Hsi-Fu by seven. And so, angry, confused, nervous, and feeling very, very foolish, I started to run down Yonge Street. I heard Sue's voice saying, "Henri, it's too much...."

Then it happened: something striking me, a strange dark sound going through my body, a sharp pain in my back, stumbling, falling on the pavement, attempts to cry out. I found myself thinking: "Did the driver who hit me notice, or is he driving on as if nothing happened?" But another thought emerged, much deeper and stronger: "Everything has changed. None of my plans matter anymore. It is awful, painful... but maybe very good." Sue's words were there: "It's too much, far too much." Then there was nothing. Just me... lying helpless on the side of the road. That feeling of powerlessness, of being completely out of control, did not frighten me. I felt as if some strong hand had stopped me and forced me into some kind of necessary surrender.

31

As I lay there, I tried to get the attention of the two gas station attendants. But they were too far off either to see or to hear me. Then, to my surprise, a young man came running toward me. He bent over me and said, "Let me help you, you've been hurt." His voice was very gentle and friendly. He seemed like a protecting angel. "A passing car must have hit me," I said. "I don't even know if the driver noticed." "It was me," he replied. "I hit you with my right mirror, and I stopped to help you.... Can you stand up?" "Yes, I guess I can," I said, and with his help, I got on my feet. "Be careful," he cautioned, "be very careful." Together we walked toward the gas station.

"My name is Henri," I said. "I'm Jon," he answered. "Let me try to get you an ambulance." We entered the gas station, and Jon put me in a chair and grabbed the phone. The two attendants looked on from a distance but said nothing. After a minute, Jon grew impatient. "I can't get through to the ambulance service. I had better take you to York Central Hospital myself." While he went out to get his van, I called Sue to tell her what had happened. A minute later we were on our way.

Looking out of the right door window, I saw the twisted mirror and realized how hard I had been hit. Jon was obviously shaken. He asked, "Why were you standing along the road?" I didn't want to explain too much but said, "I am a priest living in a community with mentally handicapped people, and I was on my way to work in one of our houses." With noticeable consternation in his voice, he said, "O my God, I hit a priest. O my God." I liked Jon and tried to console him somewhat. "I am really grateful to you for taking me to the hospital, and when I am better, you must come to visit our community." "Yes, I'd like to," he said, but his thoughts were elsewhere.

The Hospital

As soon as we reached the emergency room of the hospital, we were surrounded by nurses, doctors, a policewoman, questions and answers, admission forms, and X rays. People were extremely friendly, efficient, competent, and straightforward. The doctor who looked at the X rays said, "You've broken five ribs. We'll keep you here for a day and then let you go home." Then, unexpectedly, a very familiar face appeared. It was my G.P., Dr. Prasad. I was surprised at how quickly she had come. Seeing her gave me a deep sense of being in good hands. But at that very moment I started to feel terribly sick. I became quite dizzy and wanted to vomit but couldn't. I noticed some consternation around me, and within a few minutes it became clear that I was a lot worse off than I had thought. "There is some internal bleeding going on," said Dr. Prasad. "We must keep a close watch on you."

After many tests, tubes, and talks, I was taken to the intensive care unit. Jon had left. Sue, who had been unable to leave the house because of the ice, had called Robin, one of the members of our community, to go see me. He came, and then left to let people know what was going on. Now I was able to let the truth sink in. I was very sick and even in danger of losing my life. Faced with the possibility of dying, I realized that the mirror of the passing van had forced me to look at myself in a radically new way.

Except for brief, insignificant illnesses, I had never been in a hospital bed. But now, suddenly, I had become a real patient, totally dependent on the people around me. I could do nothing without help. The tubes going into my body at different places for intravenous injections, blood transfusions, and heart monitoring were evidence that I had become truly "passive." Knowing my very impatient disposition and aware of my need to stay in control, I expected this new situation to be extremely frustrating. But the opposite occurred. I felt quite safe in my hospital bed with its railings on both sides. Notwithstanding the severe pain, I had a completely unexpected sense of security.

The doctors and nurses explained every move they made, gave me the name of each medicine they injected, warned me beforehand of upcoming pain, and expressed their confidence as well as their doubts about the effects of their actions. During the ultrasound scan, the nurse showed me how my spleen appeared on the screen and pointed out where it was injured and most likely bleeding. The nurse who gave me Demerol to lessen the pain and help me sleep said,

"It will work for two hours, then there will be some pain again, and you will have to wait for an hour before I can give you another shot."

This directness, openness, friendliness, and levelheadedness removed my anxiety and also strengthened my ability to cope with the situation. Yes, I knew I was in danger of losing my life, but I was in the best possible place. The combination of compassion and competence took away all my fear. Most of all, the simple fact that I was treated with so much dignity and respect by people whom I didn't know and by whom I was not known made me feel very safe. I was totally dependent but was treated by everyone as an intelligent adult from whom no secrets were withheld. I was permitted to know everything I wanted to know, and in that way I kept complete ownership of my own body. Never did I sense that judgments or decisions were made concerning me without my somehow being made part of them. This gave me a deep feeling of belonging, yes, even of at-homeness. I do not have many conscious memories of being so completely cared for and, at the same time, of being taken so seriously. Perhaps it was this that filled me with such a profound sense of security.

Sue came to see me soon and during the following days became my main link with the outside world. She connected me with the Daybreak community, told me of the concern of my friends, assured me of their prayers, and kept me informed about the many small daily events at home. Her frequent visits were very comforting. We spoke a little, prayed much, and were silent for long periods.

I have to say all of this in order to explain why it was that death did not frighten me. I knew that my spleen was still bleeding and that I was still in critical condition, but no panic, anguish, fear, or worry overwhelmed me. I was surprised by my reaction. At so many moments in the past, I had experienced immense interior anguish and turmoil. I had lived through agonizing feelings of rejection and abandonment and had known paralyzing fear and panic—often triggered by small matters. I had been afraid of people and unknown forces. I knew myself as a very tense, nervous, and anxious person. Yet now, in the face of death, I felt only peace, joy, and an all-pervading sense of security.

The Surgery

B Y SEVEN O'CLOCK THAT EVENING, after many more tests, Dr. Barnes, the surgeon, said, "Your spleen is still bleeding. We have to take it out." "When?" I asked, and he said, "As soon as the operating room is free." A little later Dr. Prasad came to see me. Again I felt the threat of death. So I said to her, "If I am close to death, please let me know. I really want to prepare for my death. I am not afraid to die, but I worry about leaving life unaware." She replied, "As far as I know, there is no real danger that you will die. But we have to stop your bleeding, and so we have to remove your spleen. You will be fine within a few months, and you will be able to live well without your spleen."

45

Dr. Prasad was very honest and direct. She told me all she knew. I, myself, however, kept feeling that dying was quite possible and that I had to prepare myself and my friends for it. Somewhere, deep in me, I sensed that my life was in real danger. And so I let myself enter into a place I had never been before: the portal of death. I wanted to know that place, to "walk around" it, and make myself ready for a life beyond life. It was the first time in my life that I consciously walked into this seemingly fearful place, the first time I looked forward to what might be a new way of being. I tried to let go of my familiar world, my history, my friends, my plans. I tried to look not back, but ahead. I kept looking at that door that might open to me and show me something beyond anything I had ever seen.

What I experienced then was something I had never experienced before: pure and unconditional love. Better still, what I experienced was an intensely personal presence, a presence that pushed all my fears aside and said, "Come, don't be afraid. I love you." A very gentle, nonjudgmental presence, a presence that simply asked me to trust and trust completely. I hesitate to speak simply about Jesus, because of my concern that the Name of Jesus might not evoke the full divine presence that I experienced. It was not a warm light, a rainbow, or an open door that I *saw* but a human yet divine presence that I *felt*, inviting me to come closer and to let go of all fears.

My whole life had been an arduous attempt to follow Jesus as I had come to know him through my parents, friends, and teachers. I had spent countless hours studying the Scriptures, listening to lectures and sermons, and reading spiritual books. Jesus had been very close to me, but also very distant; a friend, but also a stranger; a source of hope, but also of fear, guilt, and shame. But now, when I walked around the portal of death, all ambiguity and all uncertainty were gone. He was there, the Lord of my life, saying, "Come to me, come."

I knew very concretely that he was there for me, but also that he was embracing the universe. I knew that, indeed, he was the Jesus I had prayed to and spoken about, but also that now he did not ask for prayers or words. All was well. The words that summarize it all are Life and Love. But these words were incarnate in a real presence. Death lost its power and shrank away in the Life and Love that surrounded me in such an intimate way, as if I were walking through a sea whose waves were rolled away. I was being held safe while moving toward the other shore. All jealousies, resentments, and angers were being gently moved away, and I was being shown that Love and Life are greater, deeper, and stronger than any of the forces I had been worrying about.

One emotion was very strong—that of homecoming. Jesus opened his home to me and seemed to say, "Here is where you belong." The words he spoke to his disciples, "In my Father's house there are many places to live in....I am going now to prepare a place for you" (John 14:2), became very real. The risen Jesus, who now dwells with his Father, was welcoming me home after a long journey.

This experience was the realization of my oldest and deepest desires. Since the first moment of consciousness, I have had the desire to be with Jesus. Now I felt his presence in a most tangible way, as if my whole life had come together and I was being enfolded in love. The homecoming had a real quality of return, a return to the womb of God. The God who had fashioned me in secret and molded me in the depths of the earth, the God who had knitted me together in my mother's womb, was calling me back after a long journey and wanted to receive me as someone who

49

had become child enough to be loved as a child. I speak only for myself here, and I simply trust that I had a very clear vision in the face of death.

Still, there were resistances to the call to come home. I spoke to Sue about them during one of her visits. What most prevented me from dying was the sense of unfinished business, unresolved conflicts with people with whom I live or had lived. The pain of forgiveness withheld, by me and from me, kept me clinging to my wounded existence. In my mind's eye, I saw the men and women who aroused within me feelings of anger, jealousy, and even hatred. They had a strange power over me. They might never think of me, but every time I thought of them I lost some of my inner peace and joy. Their criticism, rejection, or expressions of personal dislike still affected my feelings about myself. By not truly forgiving them from the heart, I gave them a power over me that kept me chained to my old, broken existence. I also knew that there were still people angry with me, people who could not think about me or speak about me without experiencing great hostility. I might not even know what I had done or said to them. I might not even know who they were. They had not forgiven me but held on to me in their anger.

In the face of death, I realized that it was not love that kept me clinging to life but unresolved anger. Love, real love flowing from me or toward me, sets me free to die. Death would not undo that love. To the contrary, death would deepen it and strengthen it. Those whom I love dearly and those by whom I am loved dearly may mourn my death, but their bonds with me will only grow stronger and deeper. They would remember me, make me part of their very members, and thus carry my spirit with them on their journey.

No, the real struggle was not a matter of leaving loved ones. The real struggle had to do with

51

leaving behind me people whom I had not forgiven and people who had not forgiven me. These
feelings kept me bound to the old body and
brought me great sadness. I suddenly felt an immense desire to call around my bed all who were
angry with me and all with whom I was angry, to
embrace them, ask them to forgive me, and offer
them my forgiveness.

As I thought of them, I realized that they
represented a host of opinions, judgments, and
even condemnations that had enslaved me to this
world. It almost seemed that much of my energy
had gone into proving to myself and to others
that I was right in my conviction that some people
could not be trusted, that others were using me
or were trying to push me aside, and that whole
groups and categories of people were falling short
of the mark. Thus I kept holding on to the illu-
sion that I am destined to be the evaluator and
judge of human behavior.

As I felt life weakening in me, I felt a deep desire to forgive and to be forgiven, to let go of all evaluations and opinions, to be free from the burden of judgments. I said to Sue, "Please tell everyone who has hurt me that I forgive them from my heart, and please ask everyone whom I have hurt to forgive me too." As I said this, I felt I was taking off the wide leather belts that I had worn while chaplain with the rank of captain in the army. Those belts not only girded my waist but also crossed my chest and shoulders. They had given me prestige and power. They had encouraged me to judge people and put them in their place. Although my stay in the army was very brief, I had, in my mind, never fully removed my belts. But I knew now that I did not want to die with these belts holding me captive. I had to die powerless, without belts, completely free from judgment.

What worried me most during these hours was

that my death might make someone feel guilty, ashamed, or left hanging spiritually in midair. I was afraid that someone would say or think, "I wish there had been a chance to resolve our conflict, to say what I really feel, to express my true intentions. . . . I wish, but now it is too late." I know how hard it is to live with these unsaid words and withheld gestures. They can deepen our darkness and become a burden of guilt.

I knew that my dying could be good or bad for others, depending on the choice I made in the face of it. I said again to Sue, "In case I die, tell everyone that I feel an immense love for all the people I have come to know, also toward those with whom I live in conflict. Tell them not to feel anxious or guilty but to let me go into the house of my Father and to trust that there my communion with them will grow deeper and stronger. Tell them to celebrate with me and be grateful for all that God has given me."

That was all I could do. Sue received my words with a very open heart, and I knew that she would let them bear fruit. She looked at me with great gentleness and let me know that all was well. From that moment on I gave myself over to Jesus and felt like a little chick safe under the wings of its mother. That sense of safety had something to do with the consciousness that anguish had come to an end: anguish from not being able to receive the love I wanted to receive, and from not being able to give the love I most wanted to give; anguish caused by feelings of rejection and abandonment.

The blood that I was losing in such quantity became a metaphor for the anguish that had plagued me for so many years. It too would flow out of me, and I would come to know the love that I had yearned for with all my heart. Jesus was there to offer me the love of his Father, a love that I most desired to receive, a love also that would enable me to give all. Jesus himself had lived anguish. He knew the pain of being unable to give or receive what he most valued. But he lived through that anguish with the trust that his Father, who had sent him, would never leave him alone. And now Jesus was there, standing beyond all anguish and calling me to "the other country."

Mary, the Mother of Jesus, was there too, but her presence was much less immediate. It seemed that she wanted to remain in the background. At first I was so taken by the tangible presence of Jesus that Mary scarcely came to my mind; retrospectively, though, I know she was there and gently witnessed the encounter of my heart with the heart of her Son. How often had I prayed, "Mary, Mother of God, pray for us sinners, now and in the hour of our death." I became aware that "now" and "the hour of my death" had become one, and I knew that she was there even though I did not focus on her. The pain was such that I could not pray with words, nor could I even think much. But every time the nurse put my wooden rosary in my hands I felt comfort. Touching these beads was all I could do, but it seemed all I needed to do in order to pray. No words, no thoughts, just simple touch.

When the nurses rolled me to the operating room and strapped me with outstretched arms on the operating table, I experienced an immense inner peace. As I looked at all their masked faces, I recognized Dr. Prasad. I had not expected her to be present but felt very glad she was there. It gave me a sense of being known and well cared for. Meanwhile, I wondered how they would put me under anesthesia. I asked, and the nurse said she would give me an injection. She did, and that was the last thing I remember.

It took a few weeks before Dr. Prasad told me what happened during surgery. "When I saw the spleen like an island in a sea of blood, I doubted whether you were going to survive the operation. You had lost nearly two-thirds of your blood, and we wondered if we could keep you alive. But Dr. Barnes was able to stop the bleeding and take out your spleen. He saved your life." It was clear that neither the surgeon, Dr. Barnes, nor Dr. Prasad had foreseen from the tests the gravity of the bleeding. But when I was rolled back to the intensive care unit, those who had attended the operation felt that I had narrowly escaped death. Shortly after I awoke from the anesthetic, one of the nurses said, "Well, you better be very thankful to him." I thought she meant Dr. Barnes, but when I asked, she said that it was God she meant.

Recovery

IN THE DAYS FOLLOWING SURGERY, I began to discover what it meant that I had not died and would soon recover. While Sue and many other visitors showed great joy and gratitude that I was out of danger and doing rather well, I had to face the simple fact that I had returned to a world from which I had been released. I was glad to be alive, but on a deeper level I was confused and wondered why it was that Jesus had not yet called me home. Yes, I was happy to be back among friends, but still I had to ask myself why it was better for me that I return to this "vale of tears." I was deeply grateful to know that I would be able to live longer with my family and community, but I also knew that living longer on this earth would mean more struggle, more pain, more anguish, and more loneliness. Interiorly, it was not easy to receive the many expressions of gratitude for my healing. It was impossible for me to say in words, "It might have been better for you if I had died and been allowed to let my absence bring you closer to God," and yet, my spirit was saying something like that.

My main question became: "Why am I alive; why wasn't I found ready to enter into the house of God; why was I asked to return to a place where love is so ambiguous, where peace so hard to experience, and joy so deeply hidden in sorrow?" The question came to me in many ways, and I knew that I had to grow slowly into the answer. As I live my life in the years ahead of me, the question will be with me always, and I will never be allowed to let that question go completely. That question brings me to the heart of my vocation: to live with a burning desire to be with God and to be asked to keep proclaiming his love while missing its fulfillment.

Confronting death has helped me to understand better the tension that belongs to this vocation. Clearly, it is a tension not to be resolved but to be lived deeply enough to become fruitful. What I learned about dying is that I am called to die for others. The very simple truth is that the way in which I die affects many people. If I die with much anger and bitterness, I will leave my family and friends behind in confusion, guilt, shame, or weakness.

When I felt my death approaching, I suddenly realized how much I could influence the hearts of those whom I would leave behind. If I could truly say that I was grateful for what I had lived, eager to forgive and be forgiven, full of hope that those who loved me would continue their lives in joy and peace, and confident that Jesus who calls me would guide all who somehow had belonged to my life—if I could do that—I would, in the hour of my death, reveal more true spiritual freedom than I had been able to reveal during all the years of my life.

I realized on a very deep level that dying is the most important act of living. It involves a choice to bind others with guilt or to set them free with gratitude. This choice is a choice between a death that gives life and a death that kills. I know that many people live with the deep feeling that they have not done for those who have died what they wanted to do, and have no idea how to be healed from that lingering feeling of guilt. The dying have the unique opportunity to set free those whom they leave behind.

During my "dying hours," my strongest feelings centered on my responsibility toward those who would mourn my death. Would they mourn in joy or with guilt, with gratitude or with remorse? Would they feel abandoned or set free?

Some people had hurt me deeply, and some had been deeply hurt by me. My inner life had been shaped by theirs. I experienced a real temptation to hold on to them in anger or guilt. But I also knew that I could choose to let them go and surrender myself completely to the new life in Christ.

My deep desire to be united with God through Jesus did not spring from disdain for human relationships but from an acute awareness of the truth that dying in Christ can be, indeed, my greatest gift to others. In this perspective, life is a long journey of preparation—of preparing oneself to truly die for others. It is a series of little deaths in which we are asked to release many forms of clinging and to move increasingly from needing others to living for them. The many passages we have to make as we grow from childhood to adolescence, from adolescence to adulthood, and from adulthood to old age offer ever-new opportunities to choose for ourselves or to choose for others. During these passages, questions such as, "Do I desire power or service?" "Do I want to be visible or remain hidden?" "Do I strive for a successful career or do I keep following my vocation?" keep coming up and confront us with hard choices. In this sense, we can speak about life as a long process of dying to self, so that we will be able to live in the joy of God and give our lives completely to others.

As I reflect on this in the light of my own encounter with death, I become aware of how unfamiliar this way of thinking is, not only for the people with whom I live and work but also for myself. It was only in the face of death that I clearly saw—and perhaps only fleetingly—what life was all about. Intellectually, I had understood the concept of dying to self, but in the face of death itself it seemed as if I could now grasp its full meaning. When I saw how Jesus called me to

66

let go of everything and to trust fully that by doing so my life would be fruitful for others, I could suddenly also see what my deepest vocation had always been.

My encounter with death told me something new about the meaning of my physical death and of the lifelong dying to self that must precede it. My being sent back into life and its many struggles means, I believe, that I am asked to proclaim the love of God in a new way. Until now I have been thinking and speaking from time into eternity, from the passing reality toward a lasting reality, from the experience of human love to the love of God. But after my having touched "the other side," it seems that a new witness is called for: a witness that speaks back into the world of ambiguities from the place of unconditional love. This is such a radical change that I might find it very hard, yes even impossible, to find the words that can reach the hearts of my fellow human beings. But I sense that words must emerge and awaken the deepest longing of the human heart.

I hear anew the words of Jesus to his Father: "My disciples are not of the world, even as I am not of the world.... As you have sent me into the world, so I have sent them into the world.... Sanctify them in the truth; your word is truth" (John 17:16–18). My experience of God's love during my hours near death has given me a renewed knowledge of not belonging to the world—to the dark powers of our society. This knowledge has entered more deeply into my heart and has led me to a fuller acceptance of my identity. I am a child of God, a brother of Jesus. I am held safe in the intimacy of the divine love.

When Jesus was baptized in the Jordan, he heard a voice from heaven, saying, "This is my beloved Son, with whom I am well pleased" (Matthew 3:17). These words revealed the true identity of Jesus as the beloved. Jesus truly heard that voice, and all of his thoughts, words, and actions came forth from his deep knowledge that he was infinitely loved by God. Jesus lived his life from that inner place of love. Although human rejections, jealousies, resentments, and hatred did hurt him deeply, he remained always anchored in the love of the Father. At the end of his life, he said to his disciples, "Listen: the time will come—indeed has come already—when you are going to be scattered, each going his own way and leaving me alone. And yet I am not alone, because the Father is with me" (John 16:32).

I know now that the words spoken to Jesus when he was baptized are words spoken also to me and to all who are brothers and sisters of Jesus. My tendencies toward self-rejection and self-depreciation make it hard to hear these words truly and let them descend into the center of my heart. But once I have received these words fully, I am set free from my compulsion to prove myself to the world and can live in it without belonging to it. Once I have accepted the truth that I am God's beloved child, unconditionally loved, I can be sent into the world to speak and to act as Jesus did.

The great spiritual task facing me is to so fully trust that I belong to God that I can be free in the world—free to speak even when my words are not received; free to act even when my actions are criticized, ridiculed, or considered useless; free also to receive love from people and to be grateful for all the signs of God's presence in the world. I am convinced that I will truly be able to love the world when I fully believe that I am loved far beyond its boundaries.

When I awoke from my operation and realized that I was not yet in God's house but still alive in the world, I had an immediate perception of being sent: sent to make the all-embracing love of the Father known to people who hunger and thirst for love but often look for it within a world where it cannot be found.

I understand now that "making known" is not primarily a question of words, arguments, language, and methods. What is at stake here is a way of being in the truth that tries less to persuade than to demonstrate. It is the way of witness. I must remain on the other side while being sent back. I have to live eternity while exploring the human search in time. I have to belong to God while giving myself to people.

Having touched eternity, I feel it is impossible to point toward it as though it were not already here. Jesus spoke from his intimate, unbreakable communion with the Father into the world and thus connected heaven with earth. To Nicodemus he says, "We speak of what we know, and bear witness to what we have seen" (John 3:11). Can I become like Jesus and witness to what I have seen? Yes, I can live in God and speak to the human reality. I can be at home in what is lasting and see significance in what passes away. I can dwell in the house of God and still be at home in the houses of people. Nurtured by the bread of life, I can work for justice for those who are starving to death for lack of food. I can taste the peace that is not of this world and engage myself in human struggles to establish justice and peace on earth. I can trust that I have somehow arrived and participate from there in my own and other people's ongoing search for God. I can let the experience of belonging to God be the place from which I can live the human pain of homelessness and estrangement.

There is, however, the danger of false security, of imagined clarity, yes, even of absolutism or dogmatism: the old temptation to control. Speaking from eternity into time can easily be perceived as oppressive, since answers may be offered before questions are raised. But Jesus' whole ministry was a ministry "from above," a ministry born of a relationship with the Father in heaven. All the questions Jesus raised, all the answers he gave, all the confrontations he evoked and the consolations he offered were rooted in his knowledge of the Father's unconditional love. His ministry was not oppressive, since it came from his deep experience of being unconditionally loved and was in no way motivated by a personal need for affirmation and acceptance. He was completely free precisely because he belonged not to the world but exclusively to the Father.

Jesus' ministry is the model for all ministry. Therefore speaking "from above" can never be authoritarian, manipulative, or oppressive. It has to be anchored in a love that is not only free from the compulsions and obsessions that taint human relationships, but free also to be present to human suffering in a spirit of compassion and forgiveness.

For me, the question is whether my encounter with death has freed me enough from the addictions of the world that I can be true to my vocation as I now see it "sent" from above. It clearly involves a call to prayer, contemplation, silence, solitude, and inner detachment. I have to keep choosing my "not belonging" in order to belong, my "not being from below" in order to be from above. The taste of God's unconditional love quickly disappears when the addictive powers of everyday existence make their presence felt again. The clarity of the meaning of life received on a hospital bed easily fades away when the many daily obligations return and start dominating life again.

It requires an enormous discipline to remain a disciple of Jesus, to continue to stay anchored in his love, and to live primarily from above. But the truth of the hospital experience cannot be denied, even though it seemed only a glimpse of a sun shining behind a cloud-covered sky. The many clouds of life can no longer fool me into denying that it is the sun that offers warmth and light. Jesus says, "I am the Way, the Truth, and the Life." Those words are no longer something for me to think about or meditate over. They have touched the center of my being and have become a tangible reality. From the perspective of that reality, people, things, and events are real because of their connectedness with the love and life of God, as revealed to me in Jesus.

Without this divine connection, people, things, and events quickly lose their eternal quality and become like fading dreams and fleeting fantasies. As soon as I lose touch with the God who is Truth, Life, and Light, I will become entangled again in the myriad of daily "realities" which present themselves to me as if they are of ultimate value. Without a very explicit and self-directed attempt to keep God in the center of my heart, it will not take long before the hospital experience becomes little more than a pious memory.

The way my friends reacted to my recovery caused me to reflect on how life and death are perceived in our society. Unanimously, they congratulated me on my restoration to health and expressed their gratitude that I was doing so well again. Although I was deeply grateful for their attention and affection, the encounter with God in my hours near death made me wonder whether being "better again" was indeed the best thing for me. Would it not have been preferable to have been completely set free from this ambiguous world and taken home to full communion with God? Would it not have been better to have left this mortal world and to be held ultimately safe in the incorruptible reality of God? Would it not have been better to have arrived than to remain on the road? No one who wrote me letters, called me by phone, sent flowers, or visited me seemed to think so. That did not surprise me; I would have responded to a friend's illness in the same way.

Nonetheless, I was somewhat surprised that no one even suggested that my return to the old life was not necessarily the best possible outcome of my accident. No one wrote, "To have been found not ready to be completely united with the Lord to whom you have given your life must have been a disappointment, but as your fellow traveler I welcome you back into the struggle of life." The countless liturgical texts that speak about our eagerness to live with God in eternal joy and peace are obviously not expressing our true desire. Life on this earth, painful and unhappy as it may be, seems to my friends preferable to the fulfillment of God's promises beyond the limits of our death. I do not say this with any cynicism. I know too well that I am not different from my friends. But having had a glimpse beyond the mirror of life, I now wonder if our eagerness to hold on to this life does not suggest that we have lost contact with one of the most essential aspects of our creed: the faith in eternal life.

All of this does help me in finding the true meaning of being restored to this life. I wonder more and more whether I am not given some extra years so that I can live them from the other side. Theology means looking at the world from God's perspective. Perhaps I am given an opportunity to live more theologically and to help others to do the same without their having to be hit by the mirror of a passing van.

As I am gradually restored to full health, I am discovering that Paul's dilemma—whether to honor Christ by life or by death—has become my own. The tension created by this dilemma is a tension that now lies at the basis of my life. Paul writes:

Life to me, of course, is Christ, but then death would be a positive gain. On the other hand again, if to be alive in the body gives me an opportunity for fruitful work, I do not know for which I should choose. I am caught in this dilemma: I want to be gone and be with Christ, and this is by far the stronger desire, and yet for your sake to stay alive in this body is a more urgent need. This much I know for certain, that I shall stay and stand by you all to encourage your advance and your joy in the faith, so that my return to be among you may be ample cause to glory in Christ Jesus on my account.

(Philippians 1:21–26)

As I return to normal life, I pray that these words of Paul may increasingly become my guide. Having come to realize that my death could have been a gift to others, I now know, too, that my life still to be lived is just as much a gift because both dying and living find their true meaning in the glory of Jesus Christ. Therefore, there is nothing to worry about. The risen Christ is the Lord of the living as well as the dead. To him belongs all the glory, honor, and praise. It may be that the mirror of a passing van has touched me just to remind me of that.

Epilogue

IT HAS BEEN A FEW MONTHS since I wrote down my experience in the portal of death. Looking back at it now that I am again fully immersed in the complexities of daily living, I have to ask myself, "Can I hold on to what I learned?"

Recently, someone said to me, "When you were ill you were centered, and the many people who visited you felt a real peace coming from you; but since you are healed and have taken on your many tasks again, much of your old restlessness and anxiety has reappeared." I have to listen very carefully to these words. Is the glimpse beyond the mirror, real and powerful as it was, not able to keep me focused on God when the demands of our hectic society make themselves felt once again? Can I hold on to the truth of my hospital experience?

At first glance, it seems impossible. How do I keep believing in the unifying, restoring power of God's love when all I experience is fragmentation and separation? The world I live in today seems no longer fertile soil in which the seed of grace can grow strong and bear fruit. As I look at the many bulldozers devastating the beautiful farmland around me in preparation for all the houses to be placed one beside the other like cars in a parking lot, I know that solitude, silence, and prayer have fled with the deer. Competition, ambition, rivalry, and an intense desire for power and prestige seem to fill the air. My crib in the intensive care unit and my bed on the fifth floor of York Central Hospital seemed safe and holy places compared with the chaos of urban "development."

But then there is my own community of handicapped people and their assistants. What about them? Somehow I know that they can make the impossible possible. Because in the midst of this power-hungry milieu, our community holds so much weakness and vulnerability that God continues to remind us of the love that was shown to me in the portal of death.

One of the most life-giving experiences of my last weeks in the hospital were the visits of my father, my sister, friends, and members of my community. They had time to spare. They had nothing more important to do. They could sit close to my bed and just be there. Especially the most handicapped were very present to me. Adam, Tracy, and Hsi-Fu came in their wheelchairs. They didn't say anything, but they were there, just reminding me that I am loved as much as they are. It seemed that they wanted to tell me that my experience in the portal of death was real and could be trusted, and by their silent presence they said to me that they might be able to keep me faithful to it. When Hsi-Fu visited me, he jumped up and down in his wheelchair, and when I hugged him, he covered my face with his kisses. He made the circle full. I wanted to come to him, but in the end it was he who came to me, as if to say, "Don't worry, I got my bath, but stay close to me so that you won't lose what you learned on your bed."

I have lost much of the peace and freedom that was given to me in the hospital. I regret it; I even grieve over it. Once again there are many people, many projects, many pulls. Never enough time and space to do it all and feel totally satisfied. I am no longer as centered and focused as I was during my illness. I wish I were. I yearn for it. It is a yearning I share with many busy people.

Because they have nothing to prove, nothing to accomplish, Hsi-Fu and all the weak and broken people of our world are given to me to call me back, again and again, to the place of truth that I have come to know. They have no success to achieve, no career to protect, no name to uphold. They are always "in intensive care," always dependent, always in the portal of death. They can bring me in touch and hold me close to that place in me where I am like them: weak, broken, and totally dependent. It is the place of true poverty where God calls me blessed and says to me, "Don't be afraid. You are my beloved child, on whom my favor rests."

I keep being reminded of Jesus' words: "Unless you become like little children, you will never enter the kingdom of heaven" (Matthew 18:3). I realize that my accident made me, at least for a while, like a little child and gave me a short taste of the Kingdom. Now all of the temptations to leave that childhood are here again, and I am not surprised that some of my friends feel that I had more to give when I was sick than after my recuperation. However, I can no longer sit and wait for another accident to point me toward the Kingdom once again. I simply have to open my eyes to the world in which I have been placed and see there the people who can help me over and over again to become a child. I know for sure that my accident was nothing but a simple reminder of who I am and of what I am called to become.

Preparing for Death

In April 1992, Henri Nouwen experienced a serious infection. This excerpt comes from notes he made for a talk given after that second brush with death.

"**C**ONGRATULATIONS," said the nurse when I woke up from the surgery after my accident. "For what?" I asked. She said, "You just made it, you are very lucky. Congratulations!"

I could have died but I didn't.

A few years later I was in the hospital again. "It's a dangerous infection you have," my doctor said. "We want to keep you alive a little longer, so you better listen to me and stop being so busy!" I had made it again! But was this what it is about? Playing Russian roulette until the bullet hits your brains? Maybe I can live another ten, twenty, or even thirty years. But is that the most important thing, or are these near-death events telling me to prepare myself for death? Death is a certainty. All other things about my future are uncertain. Still I act as if death is the least certain event of my life. I ignore it, don't speak much about it, and keep putting all my energies into the many things I still can do.

I really do not want to keep playing games with myself or with my friends. Death is all around me. Many people who were born in the year I was born have already died, and most people don't even live as many years as I have so far. Friends are dying from cancer, from AIDS, by sudden accidents. And when I enlarge the circle and look beyond my own little milieu, I see thousands and thousands of children and adults dying every day, from starvation, violence, and war. Are we prepared for death?

If we believe that death is the end, nothingness, the stopping of our clock, there is not anything to prepare for. The only thing to do is to stay alive as long and as well as possible. But I don't believe that death is the end.

All that I have learned through life and all that I experienced during my encounters with death has taught me that death is like a second birth, leading me to a new way of living. I had nothing to say about my first birth. But I have a lot to say about my second birth and I can get ready for it.

I say all of this so directly and so freely because I believe. I believe that my life, whether it is short or long, is a gift from God. I believe that God, who has given me my life, loves me with an everlasting love. I believe that this everlasting love is stronger than death, and I believe that everything that happens during my life offers me an opportunity to let my death become a rebirth.

Henri Nouwen Literary Centre
11339 Yonge Street
Richmond Hill, Ontario L4S 1L1
nouwencentre@nouwen.net
www.nouwen.net

ALSO BY

HENRI J. M. NOUWEN

SABBATICAL JOURNEY
The Diary of His Final Year

In September 1995 Henri Nouwen embarked on a spiritual adventure. He took a year's sabbatical from Daybreak, the community for the mentally and physically handicapped where he lived and served, to write, pray, and visit family and friends. Little did he know that his odyssey would find his friends multiplying, family drawing closer, and other opportunities to express kindness so present that he had little time to write at all.

Sabbatical Journey records the flowering of friendship and prayer during Henri's final year. Wherever he goes, he is aware of goodness, even amid difficult experiences such as the loss of his beloved friend Adam. To read his journal is to become his companion for a year.

Support your local bookstore or order directly from the publisher at
www.CrossroadPublishing.com

To request a catalog or inquire about quantity orders, please e-mail
sales@CrossroadPublishing.com

crossroad